ABOUT THE AUTHOR

One of four children, Steph lives in Hampshire with her two cats, Pickles and Asher. She has lived independently for 39 years, and although illness has got in the way many times, has still managed to hold down various jobs, the main one being nursing, where she qualified as a State Enrolled Nurse in 1980.

She has raised money for various charities including the Samaritans and MIND. Her hobbies include watercolour painting, knitting and listening to music.

Steph is 65 years old but not ready to retire yet!

STEPH CHAPLEN

And I'm Still Waiting!

AUSTIN MACAULEY PUBLISHERS™

LONDON • CAMBRIDGE • NEW YORK • SHARJAH

A CIP catalogue record for this title is available from the British Library.

ISBN 9781398496880 (Paperback)
ISBN 9781398496897 (ePub e-book)

www.austinmacauley.com

First Published 2022
Austin Macauley Publishers Ltd
1 Canada Square
Canary Wharf
London E14 5AA

DEDICATION

This book is dedicated to all my supporters.

ACKNOWLEDGEMENTS

I would like to thank the following:

My mum for her devoted love and for trying to understand me

My aunty and cousin for listening and believing in me

My two cats Pickles and Asher for their love even in the face of adversity

Parkway Centre, Crisis line, A & E, Hampshire Ambulance and Police, MIND, Samaritans and Rape Crisis for help and support

Leigh Park library for help with computing and printing

Positive Pathways for activities and support

Recovery College for their informative courses

My neighbours for looking after my cats

Friends and acquaintances I have met through MIND, cafés, etc.

My friend for all the CDs.

Music that has inspired me: Elton John, Queen, Carpenters, Dolly Parton, Neil Sedaka, Paloma Faith. My heartfelt thanks.

Me with Mum and Dad.

FOREWORD

FOR MOST OF the past 40 years, I've been fighting. There were times when I thought, 'To hell with it, I don't want to fight anymore, I've had enough!' But I think deep down, I always knew that that would solve nothing, and if I didn't stick around I'd never find out how it might turn out. So I suppose that glimmer of hope kept me going every time.

Much of my support has come from the psychiatric services and I don't regret one little bit anything I have shared with them. I've always had the saying, 'A problem shared is a problem halved' and I believe this to be true.

Now back on medication (and realising that I do need it), life is beginning to look up. Out with the old and in with the new.

Music has always played an important part in my life and I have included the names of some of songs that have inspired me.

Finally, I'm ready to reveal myself and tell of my incredible journey through tears, laughter, heartache, despair and joy.

CHAPTER ONE

Living in a chaotic world

FOR A FEW years, I was diagnosed with just depression but despite trying every medication available, nothing seemed to have a lasting effect. I had never been given a 'label' as such, although this might have helped me come to terms with my mood swings.

For me, the worst aspect of having a mental health problem was the unpredictability of my moods, which in effect stopped me from engaging in gainful employment. Sometimes all I needed was a 'sounding board', to verbalise things that were churning around in my head and often just hearing myself saying things helped me sort them out. Other times I needed support sorting out how much medication to take, for example, when I was 'high', until I got used to doing it for myself.

Insecurity was a major problem for me, in as much as it took me three years to accept that anyone could care what happened to me. I finally took this on board. It was not only the insecurity of not being able to trust, but also of not knowing what to do with myself, mostly when I felt depressed, but sometimes when I was 'up in the clouds' and losing touch with reality.

I still have dependency needs usually when I am 'low', but I am beginning to be more independent with my emotional feelings.

When I look back over the years, I notice particularly a strength deep inside myself which gets me through the challenges of everyday life. Allowing myself to be 'pissed off' when things get too much and congratulating myself when I manage a 'crisis' without running to the phone, is a must! There is definitely something to be said about the 'healing process'. I truly believe it is possible to overcome anything, if the determination is there in your head! And I'm not just saying this from a 'mental health' point of view.

Sometimes when I'm with my nephews and niece. I'd think, 'These are the adults of the future and how we shape their little worlds now, will affect them for the rest of their lives.' If I ever failed them in any way, it would not be for want of trying. I think 'mental health' should be taught in schools from a very early age. We are all children at heart, but if children are to grow into secure adults, they need to know that it is OK to say how they feel. None of us lives in a perfect world, but what children learn from the time they are born can shape how they feel in the world throughout their lives. Life is a learning process.

If I had a bit of money, not a lot, I would firstly send all the mental health workers on a long cruise, because I believe they have earned it. Then I would set up a complex, where anyone who wasn't able to manage the 'demons' in their head, could come and just 'be'. Just 'being' is difficult for some. This is certainly true of me. This complex would be a 24-hour affair, any time, day or night, staffed by people who had 'been there' and no questions asked. A place for people to escape and find inner peace.

Sometimes my view of the world had been distorted, I can see that now. Like living in a nightmare world for a while, frightened of everything, not being able to distinguish between fact and fiction, but all the time not wanting to give up. Even if things got too tough. And relying on that person on the end of the phone, just there at the right time. It's all in my head, well, where else would it be!?

I almost feel at peace with myself, but still feel that there is still a lot of pain inside, which needs to come out. I'm sure with all the support that I have, that I will achieve this goal.

In 2000, I had a new GP. On my first appointment, she called me 'Stephanie', which felt really nice and less formal. This was also the year I started on an injection for psychosis, which I experienced when 'high' and 'low. After being on an anti-psychotic for two years, I was able to start voluntary work in a cafe, making all the cream cakes and took part in a London competition where I won a merit award.

In 2004, I took part in a play for World Mental Health Day and that was great fun. I also started a maths course and passed level one.

I had no psychosis for over three years in total.

I have managed a few holidays away over the years on my own but never venture very far.

Written in 2004 for World Mental Health Day

Ribbons of light across a cloudy sky
Rainbows of colour
Endless seas of green and blue
All blended into one
This is my life

One day the sun will shine
For good
Well, almost
Seeing the stars hiding behind clouds
One day
The nightmare will end
There will be light
There will be warmth
From us
To stay

One day, then another
Laughter
Smiles
Heavenly peace
Well, almost

INSPIRATIONAL SONGS

'Open your heart' – Westlife
'Sad songs (say so much)' – Elton John
'What a feeling' – Irene Cara
'What a wonderful world' – Louis Armstrong
'I made it through the rain' – Barry Manilow

Me and my cousin Ginny.

My Aunty Pam. We are in regular contact and have lunch together sometimes.

My Aunty Marilyn and Uncle Bern. I'm very close to them. They are very special.

CHAPTER TWO

Relationships

I'VE NEVER BEEN any good in a relationship. They've never lasted very long. The relationship I have with my family is very distorted, mainly because of the abuse they have shown in regard to my mental health. I only really have contact with one of my siblings, but my new-found family are my dear cousin and a couple of aunties who help to support me during hard times.

My relationships with friends are strained at times, mainly because of the way I am during depressive phases. Getting angry and verbally abusive has put a lot of my friends off and many have abandoned me never to return. One friend, who sadly took her own life last year, was a constant comfort to me and forgave me time and time again. How I miss her dreadfully.

I was abused by a distant uncle at the age of eleven and this left me confused about my own sexuality. I got attached and attracted to the female psychiatric nurses that I came into contact with over the years and at one time thought I was 'Gay'.

I decided to try this out but after a 'one-night stand', I realised this wasn't for me but I was still unable to sort myself out in that area. I had a couple of boyfriends and didn't have my first serious relationship until the age of twenty. I told them about the abuse and although they were gentle and sympathetic with me, was constantly reminded about the past.

One day, I decided to go to 'Rape Crisis' and after quite a long time, was able to work through some of the feelings surrounding the abuse and lay some ghosts to rest.

I've had one relationship since then and it was OK, but that broke up years ago and I haven't found anyone to take his place.

I haven't ruled out the possibility of meeting the man of my dreams one day, but until then I'm content to continue living on my own with my two cats and lead a happy life. Well almost!

INSPIRATIONAL SONGS

'Wouldn't change a thing' – Kylie Minogue
'Reach (for the stars)' – S Club 7
'In this life' – Bette Midler
'Reason to believe' – Carpenters

CHAPTER THREE

Anger

SOMETIMES I WAS so angry, I didn't know what to do with it. I'd constantly ring 'out of hours' or the local mental health unit, but it didn't help because it just made me more angry and frustrated.

To me, anger has always meant destruction to me, mostly to myself and I normally resorted to taking an overdose of my psychiatric drugs, in an attempt to kill myself and a second later regretting what I'd done and seeking help for myself. This usually resulted in a visit to the local A & E department where they treated me and sometimes referred me to the mental health team that they have in place these days.

I think I was only angry in the first place because I felt so depressed and was wanting 'someone', 'anyone', to recognise this as a sign for help. I've lost many friends over the years because of my anger and would end up apologising when the anger left to make amends. Some were able to forgive me time and time again but many abandoned me never to return.

The professionals forgave me over and over again, but then that's what they got paid for, listening to me ranting on until there was nothing left to rant about and I eventually calmed down. I also found myself putting Bohemium Rhapsody or Rocketman DVD on full blast and at the same time music on my CD player, also on full blast. This had the desire to drown out my thoughts and the chaos in my head I don't think I've left any angry messages for quite a while now, so am finally learning to control it. I don't tend to get angry with the professionals either these days.

Recently, I went to the 'Safe Haven', a crisis centre and was given a tool to use when I feel the anger building up. I was to pick a colour and then notice anything in the flat with that colour, then move on to another colour until the anger passed. I haven't tried that yet but will bear it in mind for the future.

INSPIRATIONAL SONGS

'With a little help from my friends' – Beatles
'On my shoulder' – Westlife
'When the heartache is over' – Tina Turner
'Your song' – Elton John

CHAPTER FOUR

The Early Years

AT FIVE, I left my mother's apron strings and went to school. It was a disaster from start to finish (sweetness and light and home and Jekyll and Hyde at school).

My childhood was quite anxiety-provoking, my mind was distorted and silent distress resulted. I never got angry at home because I was frightened about how my parents would react, but at school I was always angry and often got sent out of the classroom. Looking back, I think I was just craving attention for myself as I don't think I ever got that type of attention at home.

My parents did their best for us but I think my childhood was very traumatic for many reasons. One of my sisters got angry all the time. The language that came out of her mouth was appalling and this resulted in either a beating from my dad or a bar of soap at the hands of my mum. I witnessed these distressing episodes time and time again. My brother was no better really – he never got on with my dad. They were always at war with each other and he was horrid to me which distressed me. Then there was me who spent most of their time in her bedroom alone, playing with her dolls and having fantasies with them, dreaming of a better place.

This was the norm for the house I shared with my parents, two sisters and older brother, but for Christmas and Boxing Day every year, there was a special magic that descended on our home. There were loads of presents for each of us in neat piles on the sofa and a Santa's sack on the end of our beds. My parents seemed to change into loving parents for those two days and all trauma and chaos melted away, only to return once those two days were over.

Everything changed one year when a distant uncle came to stay. I was eleven at the time. He abused me while my mum was out and told me to keep it a secret, which I did for many years. In fact, I didn't mention it to my mum till I was in my twenties. By then he was dead and I can remember wanting to dance on his grave. I don't think my mum really grasped what I was telling her. I felt free or so I thought.

After that, I had difficulty getting close to my dad or in fact any man. Every time my dad tried to hug me I can remember feeling repulsed and although he had done nothing wrong, I never felt comfortable with any sort of affection from him after that. He died in 2003 without me making amends with him. My life was never quite the same again.

At the age of sixteen, having been expelled from school with no qualifications, my mum marched me to the careers office first thing Monday morning.

My first job should have only lasted a couple of weeks, but I think my boss saw my potential and decided to keep me on. It was working as a mother's help, looking after five children (the sixth, a boy at boarding school and home for the summer holidays). The youngest (a girl) had just started school, then there was a boy of seven and three more girls aged eight, ten and thirteen.

I ran the house like a tight ship while the children were at school. Hoovering, polishing, washing (mounds of it), tidying (lots of it) – they had no sense of tidy at all! I blame their mother, my boss, for that. She never had time for them during my whole time there. She worked hard (full time) but had no love, affection or attention for her children at all. I suppose that was left up to me, but how was I to suddenly be this 'mother figure' to all those dear children?! A difficult job!

I had no idea how to deal with the children – they all seemed disturbed in some kind of way. The youngest (five years old) banged her head on the wall at night until she actually made a hole in the wall. I think they were all desperately unhappy, partly because their mother never seemed to have time for them. I looked up to her and tried to find some kind of comfort which never came, so again I was trapped in an unhappy situation. To cope I started drinking sherry and would have three or four glasses before leaving the house to do shopping, etc.

I think the children resented me because of my age and they made my life hell, but I soldiered on and stayed for four years. I started going to college and managed an 'E' grade in English Language – not much to be sniffed about in those days.

During my time as a mothers help, I joined an amateur dramatics group and excelled for the first time in acting. I enjoyed getting away from being 'me' and could take on any character. I also joined a badminton group and again was good at that and once played for the county.

In the week, I would be on my own a lot in the big house and gradually over the months, I think this is when my mood swings started to kick in. Some days I was morose and sullen but then suddenly I was like the life and soul of the party, would get on better with the children and was a joy to be around. During one depressive phase, I stopped eating and went down to six stone (I was nine before) and was taken to my boss's GP, who encouraged me to eat biscuits and drink milk! These bouts of depression and losing weight continued during my time there.

When I left at twenty, I worked in a tobacco kiosk in a local shop and was in sole charge. I did this as a stop-gap before starting my State Enrolled nurse training in 1980.

I finished my training but was constantly at Occupational health during my depressive phases and lost weight time after time. At other times when I was 'high' as I now know, I'd get on with my work but after a further period off sick, on return was told, 'Have one more bout of sickness and we will sack you'! I couldn't be certain about that so gave in my notice and that was the end of my nursing career.

INSPIRATIONAL SONGS

'Goodbye yellow brick road' – Elton John
'The climb' – Miley Cyrus
'Just because I'm a woman' – Dolly Parton
'Reach (for the stars)' – S Club 7

Me in my nurse's uniform, Christmas 1983

Mum and Dad on Christmas morning. Us four children gave them stockings filled with things from their drawers. Great fun!

With my dad, decorating Mum and Dad's house for Christmas.

CHAPTER FIVE

Hugs and Hugging

IN 1982, MY parents gave me a book called *The Little Book of Hugs*, for my birthday. I think at the time I was in hospital and although I looked at it from time to time, never really took much notice of it because I felt unhuggable at that time. My mum was never a huggy type of person, although my dad did occasionally give me a hug when I'd done something good, to praise me.

I think I only started taking notice of my own needs for a hug when I was seeing my next CPN, after my first one retired. Occasionally I would ask for a hug but it was only at her discretion and that made me feel awkward so I never asked her again. When I had my next CPN, she was lovely. I remember being traumatised when my former CPN left and she had a very difficult time with me for a long while. I remember her asking me one day what colour my eyes were because I never looked at her but at the floor. Over time, one day I did look up at her and things improved. She was very free with her hugs but I wanted them all the time because she made me feel safe and secure. 'I didn't realise you'd want so many hugs', she used to say but carried on giving them anyway.

Eventually, I felt able to ask other people who perhaps were going through a rough patch or had done something wonderful if they would like a hug. They normally said 'yes' but if they said 'no' I wasn't put off. I'd rather give them than receive them. If I was to ask for a hug these days, I feel I'd need to be in a bad place to receive one for some unknown reason. MIND have a policy of no hugs with clients. I think this is wrong because a hug can make you feel so good and improve self-esteem and mental well-being, as Kathleen Keating says in her book. I would like to change that policy if I get the chance.

Nowadays I can nurture myself. I give my cats lots of hugs (well Pickles), Asher is never so keen and in return they sort of give me a hug and that feels good. I often want to give my mum a hug but it's usually a big kiss on the cheek with my arms enfolding her but not like a hug itself. I think she loves me in her own way. She must do to have thought of buying that book all those years ago and thinking it might help me.

I'm going to have to work on allowing myself to ask for a hug, not because I'm feeling insecure and unloved but because it would be a nice thing to receive for hug's sake.

Mothers and daughters

She used to be around, but now she's gone
Somewhere else but not in this world
I'm struggling to understand, the truth is out there some-where
I can't find the words to tell her it's OK
Where have all the years gone, those happy times of old
They've all just disappeared, out of sight, out of mind

INSPIRATIONAL SONGS

'This is my life' – Shirley Bassey
'Hey whatever' – Westlife
'Heal' – Westlife

CHAPTER SIX

New Beginnings

AFTER MY NURSING career ended, I was out of work for about six years, where I attended a local day hospital (mental health) on a daily basis. I was on constant different medications and was in and out of hospital as an in-patient. My times there are very jagged but my most vivid memory was my first admission. I didn't dress, wash or do anything but sleep in every conceivable place to hide away – mostly under sofas! The decor (although I took little notice at first), was drab and dirty – the furniture old and shabby, but it was 'home' for a long while, as I began to recover. My mother used to visit in the late admissions. She may also have come on the earlier ones as well, but I have no recollection of that. She used to take me out in the car and my favourite place was always the beach, where I would sit and watch the waves lapping on the shore, over a cup of coffee.

I started to get into art work and would draw pictures of myself in coffins and other depressing places and also began writing down my feelings for the staff to read.

I remember one day mentioning to the staff that I thought I had schizophrenia – this was met with a negative response and nothing was done about it. If only they'd listened to me. My life would have been so different and I may have been able to stay in nursing with the proper medication inside me.

Soon after, I attended a rehabilitation centre and decided

on a career in secretarial work. I learnt to touch type, first on a manual then on an electronic typewriter, where my typing speeds increased enormously. On leaving the centre, embarked on a secretarial course, where despite being unwell at times, passed exams in typing, audio-typing and short-hand.

On leaving college, I got a full-time job as a 'Production Control Clerk', expediting orders and using all my powers of persuasion to get orders delivered on time. Things went really well at first but I soon became unwell again and was duly sacked after just six months. They put me through a discipli-nary hearing while I was off sick, which I felt was unfair.

Again out of work, I began to journey back to health and decided to try nursing again. This time it was working for an agency, visiting patients in their own homes. I had a car by then, but this was short-lived and my nursing career fell flat on its face again.

I was then out of work for some time. In fact, I didn't work for another eight years, living on benefits and by then having quite a lot of contact with MIND (mental health charity), attending groups attending various courses on subjects like 'self-esteem' and eventually was well enough to run a bad-minton group, which I did for four years on a weekly basis.

My family always had difficulty coping with my mood swings and time spent with them became less and less. In fact, I relied on my friends at the clubs for support. I also had regular contact with the psychiatric services during all of this time.

There were a lot of clubs to attend in the evening and although at first I only stayed for half an hour, gradually over time began to spend more time in the presence of others and over time my health improved. I was wanting to try work again but this always had a negative impact on me because of my previous history, so I stayed on benefits for years and never tried work again for quite some time.

Eventually, I decided the time was right to try work again, but after a brief full-time job with a cleaning firm, found I was unable to fulfil my commitments and left after about a year and went back on benefits. By then, I had been awarded Disability Living Allowance and this increased my financial position greatly and made it easier with my day-to-day living. I remember going out to buy furniture for my flat with some of the money and feeling quite rich at the time!

INSPIRATIONAL SONGS

'God only knows' – King & Country
'Smile' – Lily Allen
'Se a vida é (that's the way life is)' – Pet Shop Boys
'When the going gets tough' – Boyzone

CHAPTER SEVEN

'A Cry for help'

THERE HAVE BEEN many times over the years when I've needed help and support from friends and professionals, during a difficult period in my life. It has usually been the latter as they are supposed to be the experts in their field and what they get paid for. This happened during my depressive phases, when life became intolerable and I was desperate to find peace in my tormented mind.

On some occasions, life got too bad and I was looking for an easy exit away from my misery and suicide was an option for me. I tried many times to end my life, but it was never meant to be, so I struggled on regardless. I think deep down in my subconscious, there was always this voice saying, 'you are a survivor – you will get through this somehow – stick with it'. Thank God I listened to it time and time again! But it wasn't an easy ride by any means. Life was very black during those bouts and it seemed like an attractive alternative, even though I knew my death would leave a huge hole in those who care about me. But when you're in that mindset, nothing else matters except what's in your head. It takes over completely. It's a wonder I'm still here really, when I think of what I've put my body through over the years, with overdoses, sometimes almost deadly.

Just recently I tried again to end my life and decided this was it! I'd been depressed for about eight months and so having a plan in my head, I'd had the thought to mention what I intended doing. So one day, while I was waiting to see someone from MIND, left, jumped on a bus and headed for 'suicide bridge', so called because many people had jumped from there and been successful. My mobile was ringing but I ignored it. As I got off the bus it rang again. This time I answered it and it was Hampshire Police asking where I was. I tried to explain that I was in the middle of a roundabout and about to walk up the hill to the bridge.

'Stay where you are – look around you – there is a police car on its way to you.'

'What are you wearing?'

Sure enough, this police car stopped on the roundabout with its lights flashing. I was in a desperate state but so grateful that I'd been found before I'd done it for good. I shall be ever grateful for that because I wouldn't be writing this now and my friends would have lost me forever.

Since then, I have again tried to take my life. I said to someone, 'You can't help me anymore. You've tried but this is it.'

I left while waiting to see the consultant and made my way to Hayling where I intended to walk into the sea. I never made it that far and was laying on a bench when I heard sirens going past me. Not realising it was for me I stayed where I was. Hours later I was walking when a police car pulled up. They had been out looking for me and again caught me before I could come to harm.

I think it's true what they say, the quiet ones are the ones to watch because usually they have given no outward sign that that's what they intend to do. I think a lot more needs to be done to help people like that. Something in conversation, body language, just something.

INSPIRATIONAL SONGS

'Evolution' – Paloma Faith

'Crybaby' – Paloma Faith

'Break away' – Beach Boys

CHAPTER EIGHT

Untold Memoirs

I COULDN'T THINK of a better title for this next part. Great or small – they were all still a part of me and my life and something to be shared in order to move on.

My most treasured memories were the years spent with the Nautical Training Corps and St Johns Ambulance Brigade, which I did from the age of seven to sixteen. I joined the first at seven and when I was older joined the bagpipe band where I eventually became a 'pipe major' playing the bagpipes. Although I could never read music, I played 'by ear' and had a very good Scottish teacher, who would sit me down for hours teaching me tunes, which I picked up very quickly.

I thoroughly enjoyed this pastime and would spend many hours marching up and down my parent's bedroom playing my bagpipes (my bedroom wasn't big enough to march in). My brother also played in the band on the drums, but nine times out of ten we never played together! How my parents put up with the noise I'll never know!!

We had camping trips on a regular basis during the summer and these were always good fun.

Also, I enjoyed St John's, where I attained various certificates in first aid, home nursing, etc. I used to love doing beach hut duty on a Sunday and you never knew what you were going to get through the door, usually cuts and grazes, but occasionally someone with sunstroke or something. These were happy times for me.

During my early to late teens, I was into music like the Carpenters, Gilbert O'Sullivan, Neil Sedaka, Perry Como and Simon and Garfunkel. All my friends were into the latest rave music but I never had much interest in that type. I suppose even back then I was quite depressed at times.

I had a very good friend and we went everywhere together. Two other friends joined my little world and the four of us used to have great fun together. When I left school at sixteen, I lost contact with all of them and only bumped into my best friend at a dental surgery where I was working as a dental nurse. I saw one other friend one Christmas while out with the family and we were reminded about school life and happy times. I think they all eventually married and had children but I never did. I always regretted not having children but although there were a few boyfriends over the years, none of the relationships got that far and I remain single to this day.

I had years of babysitting experience when my sisters' children came along and I thoroughly enjoyed taking them out as babies and toddlers, then when they were older had them to stay over in turn. These were happy days when we were all together as a family unit, before all the upset, mainly caused through my inability to take on employment and my family's failure to acknowledge my mental illness.

My poem

For all the pain and suffering
I've come out
The other side

Learning to live again
Contentment, happiness and perhaps love

I wrote ' One day the sun will shine'
And it has
For me, at last

INSPIRATIONAL SONGS

'Absolutely nothing's changed' – Tina Turner
'Been losing my mind' – Status Quo

CHAPTER NINE

Alcohol Abuse

I HAD MY first alcoholic drink around my sixteenth birthday – sherry. It made me feel good.

When I went to work as a 'mother's help', I started drinking there and sometimes wouldn't leave the house before I'd had a few drinks. I drank because it made me feel invincible and gave me confidence.

In my later years, I used alcohol whenever I was in difficult situations – at discos, being around young men, at friends' parties – and always ended up drunk. This I continued doing from time to time but never felt the need to seek help because I could take it or leave it.

During depressive times I drank to drown my sorrows and dull everything. It all seemed much better with a few drinks inside me but really it just made everything much worse, although I couldn't see it at the time. I can't remember when I actually stopped doing this. I think it was when I'd driven to a local psychiatric hospital during a depressive phase totally intoxicated. Security took my car keys off me and I can remember sleeping under a bush on the grounds until morning, when I retrieved my keys and drove home, probably still over the limit!!! I think this was like a wake-up call and I stopped drinking. I can remember thinking that I could not only have killed myself but someone else too and I wouldn't have been able to live with that.

CHAPTER TEN

Stigma and Prejudice

FOR MANY YEARS I have faced 'stigma' and 'prejudice' from members of my own family. Yes, my own family. They accused me of 'sponging off the state', that I should be working and really ran me down at any given opportunity. My family never grasped the seriousness of my mental illness. God knows, I've wanted to work and in fact did work when I felt able, but it never lasted very long, so after a while you give up trying.

Another place where I was discriminated against was the nursing profession. They were going to sack me if I had any more time off sick.

People can be so ignorant and dismissive of mental illness when they don't understand the impact it has on your day-to-day living, as well as the financial position of not having enough money to pay the bills. I took out loans I couldn't afford to pay back in order to get some money behind me. In fact, I'm still paying back those loans.

Society as a whole needs to be educated to accept that for some people (myself included) are unable to take up any form of work, through no fault of their own.

Nowadays, employers are not able to exclude someone because of a disability and can make provisions for certain types of work schemes.

To date, I haven't stayed well enough for long enough to take on voluntary work, let alone a paid position.

INSPIRATIONAL SONGS

'When you've got what it takes' – Carpenters
'Older' – Paloma Faith
'Make your own kind of music' – Paloma Faith
'Look to your dreams' – Carpenters
'Don't go breaking my heart' – Elton John and Kiki Dee

CHAPTER ELEVEN

The Road Ahead

IN 2018, I started courses with the Recovery College (run by people who have experienced mental distress) and have now completed many courses, ranging from 'My Recovery Story', 'Talking and Listening', 'Regaining Control – Taking Personal Responsibility', 'What Is This Thing Called Self Management?', 'Taking Control of your Wellness', 'Getting Your Needs Met' and 'Overcoming Obstacles'. I am now doing a course on developing a Wellness Recovery Action Plan (WRAP) for my continued recovery and well-being. I am also hoping to do some work with MIND, as I feel I have outgrown the groups and am now ready to give something back and help others going through mental distress.

I have held a Suicide Awareness event recently and raised £86 for the Samaritans. This was mainly aimed at promoting awareness and encouraging others to look after their own mental health. I'm hoping to hold a similar event in March 2022 to spread the word.

In May 2019, I sent my article 'My Journey to Hell and Back' to the local paper. To my delight, it went in and there were also articles from other services as well. My main aim for doing this was to highlight to ordinary people the importance of looking after your own mental health and for anyone experiencing mental distress to seek help. If it only reached one person it was worth it.

When I look back over my years under the psychiatric services, I feel it has been a learning curve, especially when just recently I was finally diagnosed with Schizoaffective Disorder. At first, it felt like a death sentence but now I think I've always had this illness and wonder sometimes how my life might have turned out had I had the correct diagnosis years ago. Perhaps nothing would have changed.

I'm now in my sixty-fourth year but still learning about myself all the time. I think with age comes a maturity of coping with everyday situations, hopefully in a more positive way.

I've struck up a friendship with a fella and he makes me happy. It's early days yet but maybe he's the man of my dreams – the one I've been searching for. I think he feels the same way but we've both been hurt in the past so are taking it one step at a time.

I'm looking forward to a new chapter in my life, full of expectations, juggling 'high' and 'low' moods with normality. Daunting, but I'm sure with my determined attitude I can make something of the rest of my life on this earth. Sometimes the future scares me but I always try not to look too far into the future – just live in the here and now. None of us knows   what's around the corner, so it's best just to go with the flow and plod on regardless. And what am I waiting for? – a better life? – no, a peaceful life.

I lost my way but found it again
I've been searching for something
That was inside me already
All those years of pain
Subsiding at last

INSPIRATIONAL SONGS

'Where do I go from here' – Carpenters

'It's going to take some time' – Carpenters

'Reason to believe' – Carpenters

'Malibu' – Miley Cyrus

'The Climb' – Miley Cyrus

'Lovin' each day' – Ronan Keating

'When you say nothing at all' – Boyzone

'Reach (for the stars)' – S Club 7

'I made it through the rain' – Barry Manilow

'Suddenly' – Olivia Newton-John & Cliff Richard

'Goodbye yellow brick road' – Elton John

Asher.

Pickles.

This is my second cousin Ellie at her graduation, aged four and a half (15 July 2022).

My fella Vernon. He makes me happy and puts a smile on my face when I see him.

APPENDIX

About Schizoaffective Disorder

General Rights

I have the right to express myself provided I do not set out to hurt or put others down in the process.

So does everyone else

I have the right to be treated with respect as an intelligent capable and equal human being

So does everyone else

I have the right to state my own needs and priorities as a person whatever other people expect of me because of my roles in life.

So does everyone else

I have the right to deal with people without having to make them like or approve of me.

So does everyone else

I have the right to express my opinions and values.

So does everyone else

I have the right to ask for what I want.

So does everyone else

I have the right to say 'yes' or 'no' for myself.

So does everyone else

I have the right to change my mind.

So does everyone else

I have the right to say 'I don't understand'.

So does everyone else

I AM ME

My Declaration of Self-Esteem

IN ALL THE world, there is no one else exactly like me. Everything that comes out of me is authentically mine because I alone chose it – I own everything about me, my body, my feelings, my mouth, my voice, all my actions, whether they be to others or to myself – I own my fantasies, my dreams, my hopes, my fears – I own all my triumphs and successes, all my failures and mistakes – Because I own all of me, I can become intimately acquainted with me – By so doing I can love me and be friendly with me in, all my parts – I know there are aspects about myself that puzzle me, and other aspects that I do not know – But as long as I am friendly and loving to myself, I can courageously and hopefully look for solutions to the puzzles and for ways to find out more about me – However I look, and sound, whatever I say and do, and whatever I think and feel at a given moment in time js authentically me – If later some parts of how I looked, sounded, thought and felt turn out to be unfitting, I can discard that which is unfitting, keep the rest and invent something new for that which I discarded – I can see, hear, feel, think, say, and do. I have the tools to survive, to be close to others, to be productive, and to make sense and order out of the world, of people and things outside of me – I own me, and therefore I can engineer me – I am me and

I AM OKAY...

What is Schizoaffective Disorder?

Schizoaffective Disorder is a mental illness that can affect your thoughts, mood and behaviour. You may have symptoms of bipolar and schizophrenia. These symptoms may be mania (high mood), depression (low mood) and psychosis (losing touch with reality). About 1 in 200 people develop schizoaffective disorder at some time during their life. It tends to develop during early adulthood and is more common in women than men.

Schizoaffective Disorder has symptoms of schizophrenia and bipolar. You can experience psychosis with mania and depression. No one knows what causes Schizoaffective Disorder.

Research shows that genetic and environmental factors can increase your risk of getting this Illness.

Diagnosis and Symptoms

A psychiatrist will diagnose Schizoaffective Disorder after a mental health assessment. It might take more than one assessment for the psychiatrist to reach a diagnosis. You may get a diagnosis of Schizoaffective Disorder if you have depressive or mania symptoms with symptoms of schizophrenia. To get a diagnosis of Schizoaffective Disorder you should have had a combination of symptoms of both psychosis and bipolar disorder. Your symptoms should be clearly there for at least two weeks.

Symptoms of Schizophrenia

Schizophrenia is a mental illness which affects the way you think. Symptoms can affect how you cope with day-to-day life. Symptoms include:-

- Hallucinations – you may hear, see or feel things that aren't there

- Delusions – you may believe things that aren't true

- Disorganised speech – you may begin to talk quickly or slowly and things you say may not make sense to other people. You may switch topics with no obvious link

- Disorganised Behaviour-you might struggle to organise your life or stick to appointments, etc.

- Catatonic Behaviour – you may feel unable to move or appear to be in a daze

- Negative symptoms – these are symptoms that involve loss of ability and enjoyment in life. They can include the following things:
  - Lack of motivation
  - Change in sleep patterns
  - Poor grooming or hygiene
  - Difficulty in planning and setting goals
  - Not saying much
  - Change in body language
  - Lack of eye contact
  - Reduced range of emotions
  - Less interest in socialising or hobbies and activities
  - Low sex drive

What are the symptoms of Mania?

You may experience the following if you have mania:

- Feeling overly active or energetic or restless

- Feeling more irritable than usual

- Feeling overly confident

- Talking very quickly, jumping from one idea to another or having racing thoughts

- Feeling elated, even if things are not going well for you

- Being easily distracted and struggling to focus on 1 topic

- Not needing much sleep

- Thinking you can do more than you can, which could lead to risky situations and behaviour

- Doing things you wouldn't normally which can cause problems, such as spending lots of money, having casual sex with different partners, using drugs or alcohol, gambling or making unwise business decisions

- Being much more social than usual

- Being argumentative, pushy or aggressive

Mania is associated with Bipolar Disorder.

What are the symptoms of Depression?

You may experience the following:

- Low mood

- Less energy, tired or 'slowed down'

- Hopeless or negative

- Guilty, worthless or helpless

- Less interested in things you normally like to do

- Difficulty concentrating, remembering or making decisions

- Restless or irritable

- Sleep too much, not being able to sleep or have disturbed sleep

- More of less hungry than usual or have a weight change

- Thoughts of death or suicide or attempted suicide

Types and Causes

There are three different types of Schizoaffective Disorder.

What is the manic type?
This means you have symptoms of schizophrenia and mania at the same time through a period of illness

What is the depressive type?
This means you have symptoms of schizophrenia and depression at the same time through a period of illness

What is mixed type?
This means you have symptoms of schizophrenia, depression and mania at the same time through a period of illness

What causes Schizoaffective Disorder?

Psychiatrists don't know precisely what causes Schizoaffective Disorder, but we do know that you will have a chemical imbalance in your brain if you have the condition.

Research shows that genetic and environmental factors can increase your risk of developing the illness.

Genetic Factors
Schizoaffective Disorder is slightly more common if other members of your family have Schizophrenia, Schizoaffective Disorder of Bipolar Disorder.

Environmental Factors

These are your personal experiences. It is thought that stress can contribute towards a schizoaffective episode. Stress can be caused by many things such as bereavement, debt or employment problems. Childhood trauma can also be a factor in the condition developing in later life. Research suggests that bad treatment in your childhood can make psychosis more likely.

Who will manage my treatment?

Different mental health teams can support and treat you.

Referrals

A doctor can refer you to a mental health professional if deemed necessary or you can refer yourself.

What is an NHS Community Mental Health Team (CMHT)?

This is a team of professionals who support you to recover from mental health issues. They can give short or long-term care in the community.

What is an NHS Crisis Team?

They can support you if you are having a crisis in the community. They can offer short-term support to help prevent hospital admissions. They can arrange for you to go to hospital if you are very unwell.

You can get crisis support by:

- Calling your NHS urgent mental health helpline

- Calling NHS 111 or

- Talking to your GP

Further reading

Wellness Recovery Action Plan (WRAP) plus: This is a self-designed wellness process. You can use a WRAP to get well, stay well and make your life your own. It was developed in 1997 by a group of people who were searching for ways of coping with their own lives and fulfilling dreams and ambitions.

Useful Contacts

The hearing voices network

Support and understanding for those who hear voices or experience other types of hallucination.
Address:- 86-90 Paul Street, London, EC2A 4NE
Email:- info@hearing-voices.org
Website:- www.hearing-voices.org

Risks that Schizoaffective Disorder can cause

Suicide risk is higher for the first few years after symptoms start. You can seek treatment early and make a crisis plan. The right treatment can help control your symptoms and help lower the risk of suicide.

You can make a crisis plan yourself or ask someone to help you. This will help to deal with suicidal thoughts. Usually, a plan includes people, services and activities that can help you.

Carers

If you are a carer, you can get support if you care for someone with schizoaffective disorder.

Here are some options:

- Family intervention through NHS

- Join a carers service

- Ask your local authority for a carers assessment

- Read about the condition

- Apply for welfare benefits for carers

- Rethink Mental Illness run carers support groups in some areas.

- Also search for groups on the Carers Trust website.

Rethink Mental Illness www.rethink.org, about-us/our-support-groups

Carers Trustwww.carers.org/search//network-partners